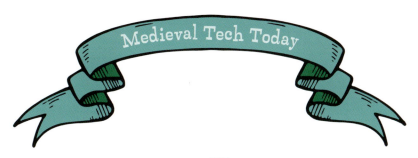

Do You LIVE Like It's MEDIEVAL Times?

Personal Technology THEN and NOW

by Megan Cooley Peterson

Content Consultant:
James Masschaele, PhD
Professor of History, Executive Vice Dean
School of Arts and Sciences
Rutgers University
New Brunswick, New Jersey

CAPSTONE PRESS
a capstone imprint

Captivate is published by Capstone Press, an imprint of Capstone.
1710 Roe Crest Drive
North Mankato, Minnesota 56003
www.capstonepub.com

Copyright © 2021 by Capstone. All rights reserved. No part of this publication may be reproduced in whole or in part, or stored in a retrieval system, or transmitted in any form or by any means, electronic, mechanical, photocopying, recording, or otherwise, without written permission of the publisher.

Library of Congress Cataloging-in-Publication Data is available on the Library of Congress website.
ISBN: 978-1-4966-8471-4 (hardcover)
ISBN: 978-1-4966-8491-2 (eBook PDF)

Summary:
From soap to pretzels, medieval innovators used technology to develop or improve items that we use in our daily lives. The Middle Ages were crucial for the improvement of chess, the compass, glasses, and more! Discover how we still live like we're in medieval times.

Image Credits
Alamy: Dembinsky Photo Associates/Mark A Schneider, 33, FLHC 16, 41, ITAR-TASS News Agency, 9, Maurice Savage, 43, Mike Booth, 18, Science History Images, 31, 35, TopFoto, 42, WBC ART, 25; Getty Images: Anadolu Agency/Contributor, 8, DEA/A. DAGLI ORTI/Contributor, 37, DEA/M. SEEMULLER/Contributor, 40, General Photographic Agency/ Stringer, 23; iStockphoto: Grafissimo, 5; Mary Evans Picture Library, 11; Newscom: akg-images, 15, 17, Danita Delimont Photography, 22, Heritage Images/English Heritage, 7, Pictures From History, 39, UIG Universal Images Group/ Encyclopaedia Britannica, 19; North Wind Picture Archives: Gerry Embleton, 13; Shutterstock: Aleksandr Pobedimskiy, 34, Andrey_Popov, 27, Cls Graphics, Cover (Bottom Right), dennizn, 32, Eric Isselee, 26, 30, faboi, 36, Gaspar Janos, 6, hecke61, 21, Isa Ismail, 28, Nitr, Cover (Bottom Left), Pranav Kukreja, 4

Design Elements
Capstone; Shutterstock: andromina, Curly Pat, derGriza, Evgeniya Mokeeva, Introwiz1, Kompaniets Taras, lightmood, ONYXprj, Tartila, yalcinart, Yana Alisovna

Editorial Credits
Editor: Michelle Parkin; Designer: Sarah Bennett; Media Researcher: Jo Miller; Production Specialist: Katy LaVigne

All internet sites appearing in back matter were available and accurate when this book was sent to press.

Table of Contents

CHAPTER 1
Back to the Middle Ages..................4

CHAPTER 2
Soap..................8

CHAPTER 3
Chess..................12

CHAPTER 4
The Mechanical Clock..................16

CHAPTER 5
The Coffee House..................20

CHAPTER 6
The Pretzel..................24

CHAPTER 7
Pest Control..................26

CHAPTER 8
The Compass..................32

CHAPTER 9
Eyeglasses..................36

CHAPTER 10
Paper Money..................40

    Timeline of Technology..................44
    Glossary..................46
    Read More..................47
    Internet Sites..................47
    Select Bibliography..................47
    Index..................48

Words in **bold** are in the glossary.

CHAPTER 1

Back to the Middle Ages

Your alarm goes off and you wake up. You stumble out of bed and get dressed. You look at the clock. It's time to go! You put on your glasses and run to catch the bus. At lunch time, you open a bag of pretzels in your lunchbox. When you get home, you play a quick game of chess online before starting your homework.

This may sound like a normal day. But did you know that many of the things we do every day started or were improved upon during the Middle Ages? People from this time period used clocks, wore glasses, played chess, and even ate pretzels.

People in the Middle Ages used early versions of some items we use today.

The Middle Ages was a time period from about AD 476 to 1500. This is also referred to as medieval times.

Medieval people grew crops, made food, played games, and went to church. Some attended school. And they also developed some useful items that we still use today. Daily life in the Middle Ages was filled with inventive people doing the best they could with what they had.

Life on a Medieval Manor

Most medieval people weren't heroic knights or wealthy **lords** living in grand castles. They were **peasant** farmers. They raised crops on land owned by lords. This land was called a manor. The peasants had to give crops or pay taxes to lords. In return, lords protected them during wars. Some peasants owned small pieces of land or rented land from lords. Peasants typically lived in small villages. Their homes were small and usually made of sticks, twigs, and **daub**.

Peasants lived in small homes with roofs made of dry straw or grass.

A lord's daily life was very different from a peasant's life. A lord lived in a large manor house protected by strong walls. The great hall was the main room inside the house. The lord hosted meals and events there. He also oversaw legal proceedings. Servants and soldiers worked and lived at the manor house. They performed all the tasks needed to make the manor run.

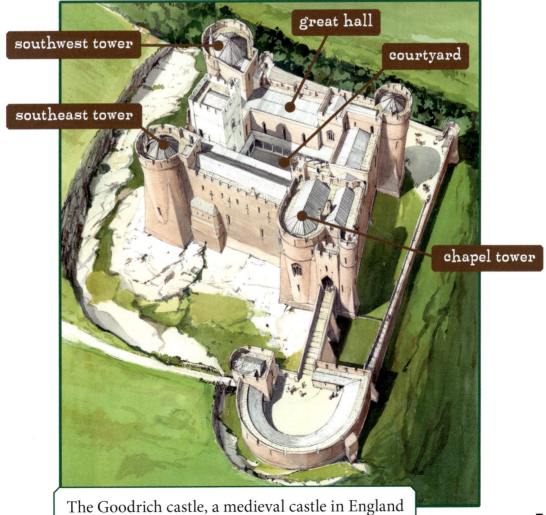

The Goodrich castle, a medieval castle in England

Soap

In 2014, a soapmaking company in Lebanon gave the first lady of Qatar a bar of soap. But it wasn't just any bar of soap. It was the most expensive soap in the world. The palm-sized bar cost $2,800. Why did it cost so much? The soap was made with oils and fragrant plants. It also had two special ingredients—gold and diamond powder.

It took one and a half months to make the expensive bar of soap.

Most soap is made from oils or animal fats, then mixed with **lye**. Lye causes a chemical reaction, which changes the fats into soap. In factories, giant batches of soap are mixed in huge cauldrons. Then the soap is sprayed onto a large metal roller. This turns the soap into ribbons. Different fragrances and dyes are added. Eventually the soap is put into molds.

Soap is pressed into molds in factories and packaged to be sold.

Soap wasn't as readily available in the Middle Ages as it is today. But staying clean was important to medieval people. Medical books from the Middle Ages talked about the importance of bathing. Most people had to make their own soap. They also found other ways to keep clean.

Soap in Medieval Europe

In medieval Europe, soap was used mostly for cleaning clothes. People boiled animal fat and wood ashes together to make lye soap. They washed clothing and floors with lye soap. It was too harsh to use on their skin.

Gentler soaps for bathing contained olive oil. An olive-oil soap made in Castile, Spain, became so popular that all soaps like it were called Castile soap. This soap was more expensive than lye soap. Most medieval people could not afford it.

Medieval people didn't bathe every day, but they kept themselves clean. They washed their heads, hands, feet, and faces each day using basins of water. At bath time, water had to be heated up using a fire. Then the heated water was dumped into a wooden tub. Family members usually took turns bathing in the same tub water.

A medieval wash room inside a castle

If the wooden tub was large enough, they bathed together while the water was still hot. Historical records show medieval people used sponges and small towels to clean and dry themselves.

∽ FACT ∽

Medieval people often picked lice off each other. In the 1200s, people were banned from picking lice in public spaces in Italy.

CHAPTER 3
Chess

Chess is one of the most popular games in the world. Two players take turns moving pieces across a grid, called a chessboard. Each piece moves around the board in a different way. The player who captures the other player's king piece in a **checkmate** wins the game. Chess takes a lot of patience. A player must try to think several moves ahead, guessing what the other player might do. It takes years of practice to master the game.

In 1989, two chess players set the world's record for the longest game of chess. Siberian players Ivan Nikolic and Goran Arsovic faced off in the Serbian city of Belgrade. The game lasted for 20 hours!

FACT
Medieval people played other board games as well, such as backgammon and checkers.

Many people in the Middle Ages played chess, including Chinese Emperor Kublai Khan (left) and explorer Marco Polo (right).

The Ultimate Board Game

Chess was a popular game during the Middle Ages as well. It may have started in India in the 500s. The game was called *chaturanga*. In the game, four players moved game pieces across a 64-square grid. When the game spread to **Persia**, the name was changed to *chatrang*. The game now was for two players. After Muslims discovered *chatrang*, they renamed it *shatranj*. To win in this version, a player had to capture all of the other player's pieces. By the early 1000s, chess had spread throughout Europe.

Chess Changes

People in Europe played the Muslim version of chess for hundreds of years. Over time, they changed the names of the chess pieces to reflect their way of life. The moves began to change as well. The queen piece was given more power on the board. A player won by capturing their opponent's king in a checkmate. By the 1600s, the modern version of chess had developed.

Chess became quite popular among nobles. They used chess to plan for wars. On special occasions, people played life-size versions of chess. They dressed up in costumes and pretended to be the game pieces!

Medieval nobles believed that playing chess made them smarter.

∽ FACT ∽

In 1841, a 700-year-old grave was discovered in Scotland. There were 78 medieval chess pieces inside the grave.

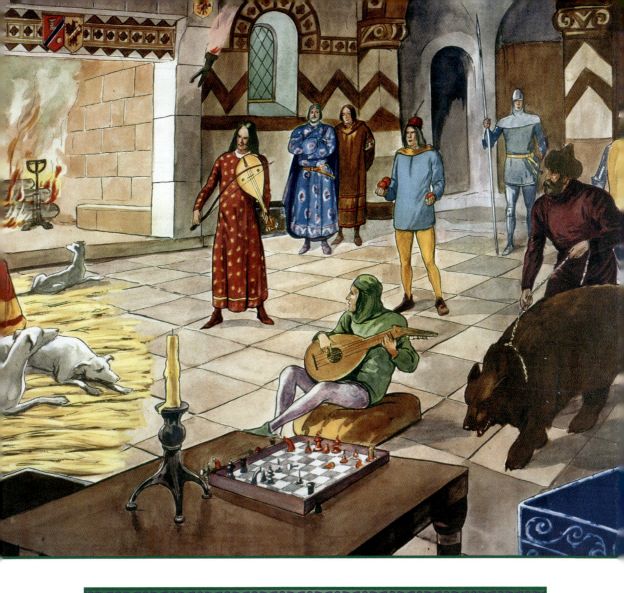

A Chess Legend

According to **legend**, chess was invented to ease a broken heart. An Indian queen's son died in a battle. The queen's advisors asked a philosopher to help them break the news to the queen. The philosopher invented the game of chess to explain how her son died.

The Mechanical Clock

Times Square in New York City turns into a party zone every New Year's Eve. Thousands of people from around the world gather to welcome the new year. Millions more watch the event on TV. A giant digital clock stands over the crowd as they watch the minutes tick closer and closer to midnight. Above the clock, a colorful ball sits atop a long pole. During the final minute of the year, the ball moves down the pole. It reaches the bottom as the clock strikes midnight.

The use of a ball to tell time goes back to at least 1833. England's Royal Observatory in Greenwich used a bright red ball to tell time. The Time Ball sits on top of the Flamsteed House and still runs today. Each day at 12:55 p.m., the ball rises halfway up the pole. Three minutes later, it reaches the top. Then at 1:00 p.m. exactly, the ball falls to the bottom of the pole. Because of its size and location, the Time Ball told ship captains at sea the precise time once each day. If needed, they could adjust their onboard clocks.

Medieval Water Clock

Time and the ability to measure it have always been important. For thousands of years, people have found different ways to keep track of time. In the early Middle Ages, the water clock was the most accurate way to tell time. The water clock was invented in Egypt around 1400 BC. Flowing water filled a container in the clock. Marks on the container showed how much time had passed. Around 270 BC, Greek inventor Ctesibius improved the water clock. His clock used a continuous flow of water to move a pointer. The pointer marked when each hour passed.

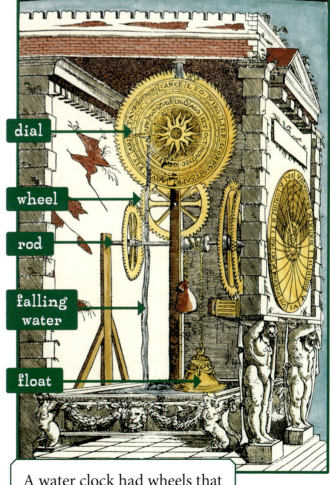

A water clock had wheels that moved when the water fell.

The Mechanical Clock

The first mechanical clocks appeared in medieval Europe in the early 1300s. They were large and had no numbers or hands to tell the time. Instead, a bell rang every hour. These clocks were used in churches and monasteries. The clock's bell signaled when it was time to pray or eat meals.

In medieval cities and towns, clocks were installed on towers to help the townspeople keep track of the time. The clock's bell told people the hour but not the minutes. Kings and nobles started putting smaller versions of these clocks in their castles in the early 1400s.

The oldest mechanical clock in England is at Salisbury Cathedral. The clock was built in 1386.

How They Worked

Early mechanical clocks were run by a series of gears and weights. A weighted **foliot** moved back and forth. As it moved, the foliot moved a toothed gear. This gear powered the clock.

Clocks grew smaller in the mid-1400s with the invention of spring-driven clocks. These clocks used smaller coiled springs instead of heavy weights. These clocks cost a lot less. Clockmakers began making smaller clocks that more people could afford.

Today, people use digital clocks, watches, and cell phones to tell time. These clocks don't need gears and springs to run.

Inside Early Mechanical Clocks

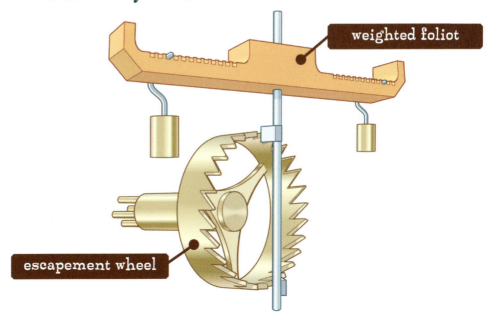

CHAPTER 5

The Coffee House

Coffee is one of the most popular drinks in the world. People often go to coffee houses to meet up with friends or do business. Most coffee shops are small. But the Al-Masaa Café in Saudi Arabia thinks bigger is better. This café has more than 1,000 seats! Coffee lovers can enjoy their coffee drinks inside or outside with amazing views of the city.

Today, it's hard to imagine a world without coffee. But throughout most of the Middle Ages, Europeans had never heard of it. Medieval people drank wine, beer, and ale.

Coffee is an important part of Ethiopian culture. The traditional coffee ceremony of roasting coffee beans and preparing boiled coffee can last two to three hours.

Coffee Houses in the Middle East

Coffee is made from the coffee plant, which is native to Africa. The first coffee plants arrived in the Middle East from Ethiopia in the 1400s. Many Muslim people enjoyed this new beverage. Since alcohol was forbidden in their religion, many Muslims chose coffee as an alternative.

As coffee's popularity grew in the Middle East, so did its importance in Muslim culture. Coffee houses, called *qahveh khaneh*s, were built. Men gathered at coffee houses to drink coffee, play games, and listen to music. They also shared ideas on many topics, including politics.

Coffee Houses in Europe

In the mid-1500s, coffee was introduced to Constantinople, in modern-day Turkey. The drink became popular quickly. Within 10 years, there were 600 coffee houses in the city. Many of them were located in lush gardens with comfortable furniture.

Did Goats Discover Coffee?

According to legend, an Ethiopian goat herder discovered coffee. One day, he noticed his goats eating berries from a tree. Soon, the goats started running and jumping around. They would not go to sleep that night. The goat herder told the head of a local monastery about the berries. This leader made a drink out of the berries—the first cup of coffee.

Lloyd's Coffee House in London became a popular spot for sailors and businessmen in the late 1600s.

Coffee houses spread more slowly throughout the rest of Europe. The first coffee house in London, England, opened in 1652. More than 30 years later, the first coffee house opened in Venice, Italy. Just as they had in the Middle East, European coffee houses became important meeting places for men to discuss business and politics.

CHAPTER 6

The Pretzel

Pretzels come in many shapes, sizes, and flavors. They can be soft and chewy or hard and crunchy. Most of these popular snacks are made in factories.

Medieval bakers created the first pretzels. No one knows for sure when the first pretzel was baked. According to one story, an Italian monk came up with the idea in AD 610. The Catholic church had strict rules about what could be eaten during Lent, a religious period. Meat, dairy, and eggs were forbidden. The monk created the first pretzel using water, flour, and salt. It was soft, not crunchy.

Medieval art shows people enjoying pretzels. People during this time thought pretzels brought good luck and prosperity.

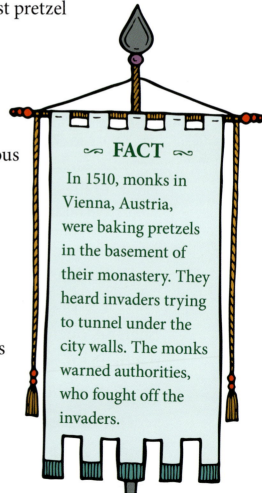

FACT

In 1510, monks in Vienna, Austria, were baking pretzels in the basement of their monastery. They heard invaders trying to tunnel under the city walls. The monks warned authorities, who fought off the invaders.

A medieval painting from around 1460 shows a pretzel on the table.

Pest Control

Cockroaches, mice, bedbugs—no one wants to come across these pests at home. But sometimes the pests find their way inside. In the wild, mice only live about a year. But give a mouse a warm, dry home with access to food, and it can live up to three years. Female mice give birth about every six weeks. This means one female mouse can have hundreds of babies in just a few years.

Today's pest-control companies work to keep homes and businesses pest free.

Today, pest control companies use traps and poisons, just as people did in the Middle Ages. However, the tools and products have changed a lot since then.

The Stinking Middle Ages

Unwanted pests were a big problem during the Middle Ages. Pests were annoying and could spread dangerous diseases.

Cities and towns were growing larger. As the population grew, so did the amount of human waste. Medieval towns didn't have sewage systems. People kept small pots, called chamber pots, in their homes. They went to the bathroom in these pots. Then they took them outside and dumped them into **cesspits**, which often emptied into rivers or streams. Sometimes people dumped full chamber pots right onto the streets. Public toilets also emptied into flowing water. In castles, bathrooms were built into the outside walls. Waste fell into **moats** or waterways below.

Medieval toilets were discovered in the Tower of London.

When people died in the Middle Ages, they were often buried up against the walls of the churches. As cities grew, the dead bodies began to pile up. Soon, there were so many bodies buried together that bones began sticking out of the dirt. They had to be dug up and moved into vaults. Decaying bodies and waste made medieval towns smell terrible. The smell attracted all sorts of pests, including rats and mice.

FACT

In Florence, Italy, medieval people produced around 5,000 tons of solid human waste each year.

A Smelly Job

Some medieval cesspits were not connected to rivers or streams. At night, workers had to shovel them out. They carted the waste to nearby rivers or streams to dump it. In Nuremberg, Germany, one of the city's cesspits hadn't been cleaned in 17 years. It took workers three nights to clear. They hauled away 108 carts full of solid waste.

Early Pest Control

Medieval people did not want pests taking over their farms and cities. They came up with all sorts of ways to get rid of the unwanted critters. People mixed together barley flour, roses, and cucumbers to try to kill mice. Ground oleander leaves were placed in holes to lure fleas away from homes.

The Black Death

From 1347 to 1351, the bubonic plague spread through Europe. This disease caused swollen lymph nodes, fever, vomiting, and eventually death. Known as the Black Death, the plague killed more than 20 million medieval Europeans. Fleas from black rats may have spread the disease to humans.

Professional rat-catching was one of the earliest forms of pest control.

Professional rat-catchers emerged during the Middle Ages. Rat-catchers used poisoned food and traps to catch the rats. A common trap in the 1200s dropped a weight onto the rat to kill it. Rat-catchers walked through towns carrying long poles with dead rats attached. This showed future customers the rat-catcher's skill at trapping pests.

∽ FACT ∽

Medieval people rubbed radish juice on their hands to pick up and remove scorpions from their homes. They believed the juice protected them from scorpion stings. It didn't.

CHAPTER 8

The Compass

Travelers today use their smartphones to get around. Almost every location on Earth can be found with a map app or quick online search. Just type in where you want to go and your phone will show you how to get there. Modern compasses have made it almost impossible to get lost. GPS navigation uses a series of satellites orbiting Earth to find locations. The satellites broadcast radio signals to GPS receivers in cars, airplanes, and smartphones.

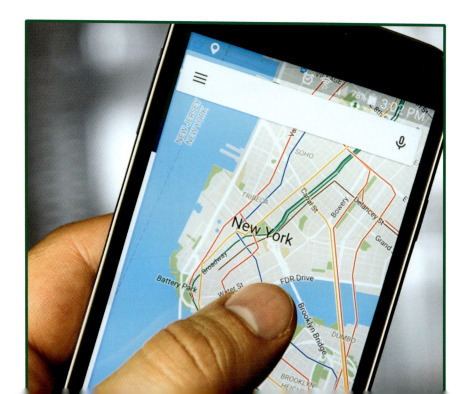

Navigation wasn't as easy in the Middle Ages. It was hard to know where you were going. European explorers had not yet traveled around the world. Maps were drawn by hand and were often wrong. Some early medieval maps showed the earth as a flat disc. Early medieval sailors used the positions of the sun and stars to guide them. They also relied on landmarks to help them navigate unknown waters.

Vikings in the Middle Ages used sunstones to navigate the seas. Sunstones were made from pieces of gemstones. When light passed through these gemstones, it changed the brightness and color of the stone. By turning these stones, Vikings could find where the sun was on cloudy days.

Vikings used gemstones such as Iceland spar to find where the sun was located.

The First Compasses

Earth acts like a giant magnet. It has a magnetic North and South Pole. A compass uses Earth's magnetic field to show direction. A free-spinning magnet inside the compass always points to Earth's magnetic North Pole.

Early magnetic compasses may have been developed in China during the Han Dynasty (200 BC–AD 200). Spoon-shaped pieces of lodestone pointed to Earth's magnetic North Pole.

By the 1100s, compasses were being developed in Europe. Medieval people discovered they could magnetize pieces of iron by rubbing them against lodestones. When the iron was placed on a stick in water, it pointed toward Earth's magnetic north. In 1269, French scientist Peter Peregrinus wrote about a dry compass with a pivoting metal pointer. He included a drawing, which had a round face marked with 360 degrees.

Medieval sailors used magnetic compasses to navigate the seas.

Chapter 9
Eyeglasses

Do you wear glasses? Look at the lenses. Most eyeglass lenses today are made from large plastic discs in factories. Workers program a customer's lens prescription into a machine, which thins and shapes the disc to the right prescription. Then another machine polishes the lens with rough paper. Eventually, the lens is cut to match the shape of the eyeglass frames.

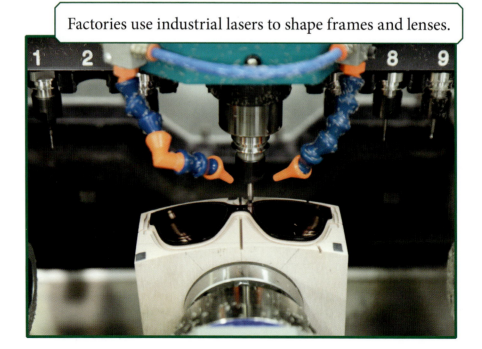

Factories use industrial lasers to shape frames and lenses.

Throughout history, people have struggled with vision problems. But they didn't have a way to see better until the Middle Ages. In the 1200s, people in Italy began making spectacles. These were the first eyeglasses. At first, spectacles used convex lenses. A convex lens is thicker in the middle and thinner around the edge. It makes objects appear larger, like a magnifying glass. People held spectacles up to their eyes or pinched them onto their noses. Early frames were made of metal, bone, or wood.

The first spectacles in Germany were made in 1350.

～ FACT ～
Spectacles were first recorded in 1267, by English philosopher Roger Bacon.

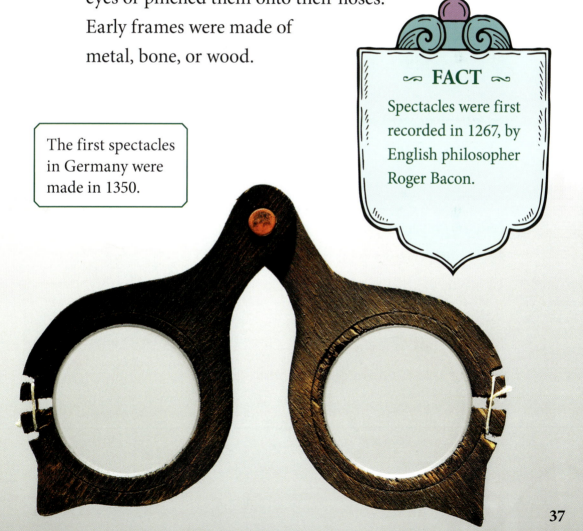

The Science of Glasses

By the mid-1400s, concave lenses were being made in Italy. Concave lenses are thinner in the middle and thicker at the edges, like an hourglass. These lenses help people see far away. Lens makers began to make lenses of different strengths, depending on the wearer's needs.

Looking into the Future

The need for glasses continued to grow after the end of the Middle Ages. By the late 1600s and early 1700s, sides were added to spectacles. Like eyeglasses today, the spectacles could rest behind the wearer's ears.

Founding Father Benjamin Franklin needed help seeing both close up and far away. He wanted a single pair of glasses that could help with both of his vision problems. In 1784, Franklin glued the top half of a concave lens to the bottom half of a convex lens. He had invented the bifocal lens.

FACT

The first contact lenses were made of glass. Today, contacts are made of a flexible plastic.

Franklin called his glasses double spectacles. Bifocals are still used today.

Eyeglasses have continued to evolve. By the late 1800s, doctors were experimenting with contact lenses. Like glasses, they correct vision but are worn directly on the eyes. Today, eyeglasses and contacts are more comfortable and stylish than ever before.

CHAPTER 10

Paper Money

The U.S. Bureau of Engraving and Printing is often called the Money Factory. The paper money you use today is designed and printed there. Steel plates print the bill's design onto special sheets of paper. Then the bills are cut down to size and bundled together.

Today's lightweight bills can easily fit into your pocket. But money in the Middle Ages was not as easy to carry around. In the early Middle Ages, people had to haul heavy loads of metal coins to buy things.

Medieval people used metal coins made of silver or gold to pay for items and rent.

During the Tang Dynasty (AD 618-907) in China, people began carrying paper money instead of coins. The paper represented a certain number of metal coins. In the 1100s, the Chinese government issued paper money called *jiaozi*.

FACT

In AD 674, the Chinese government coated its paper documents and money with poison to stop insects from eating them.

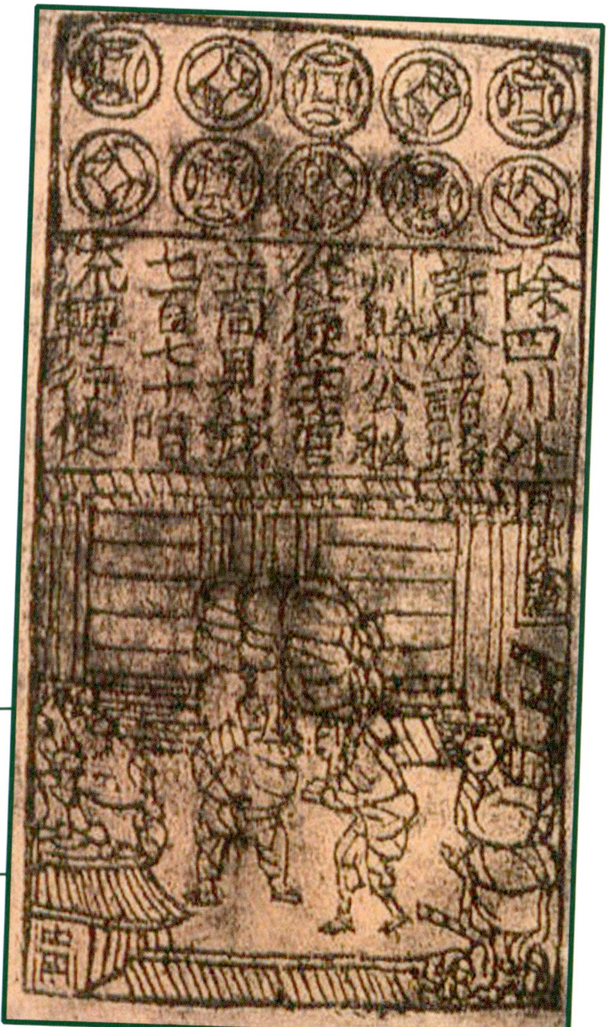

Jiaozi was the first government-issued money in history.

41

William of Rubruck wrote detailed accounts of what he observed in Mongolia.

Paper Money Comes to Europe

A European monk named William of Rubruck traveled to Mongolia from 1253 to 1255. He discovered that they used paper money made from mulberry bark. William wrote a book about his travels. Many people in Europe read it. But it still took a few hundred years for paper money to catch on in Europe.

~ FACT ~

By the late 1600s, bankers kept customers' coins safely locked away. In exchange, they issued banknotes.

In 1775, the Continental Congress issued the first banknotes in America.

Daily Life in the Middle Ages

Life in the Middle Ages wasn't easy. People didn't have electricity or running water like we do today. But their lives were not as bad as some might think. They invented and developed many tools and items we still use in our daily lives—to help us see, help us clean, feed us, and even entertain us. These items have changed and improved over the centuries. But medieval people deserve credit for inventing or advancing technologies that make our lives easier.

Timeline of Technology

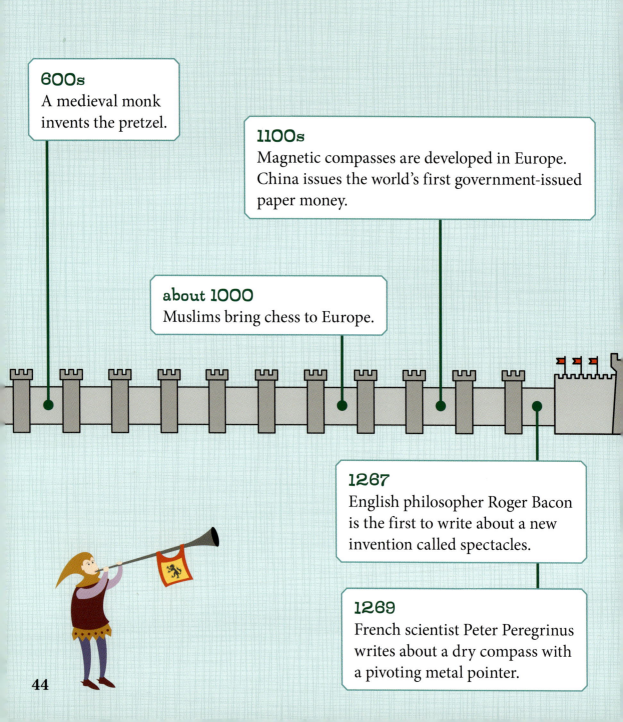

600s
A medieval monk invents the pretzel.

1100s
Magnetic compasses are developed in Europe. China issues the world's first government-issued paper money.

about 1000
Muslims bring chess to Europe.

1267
English philosopher Roger Bacon is the first to write about a new invention called spectacles.

1269
French scientist Peter Peregrinus writes about a dry compass with a pivoting metal pointer.

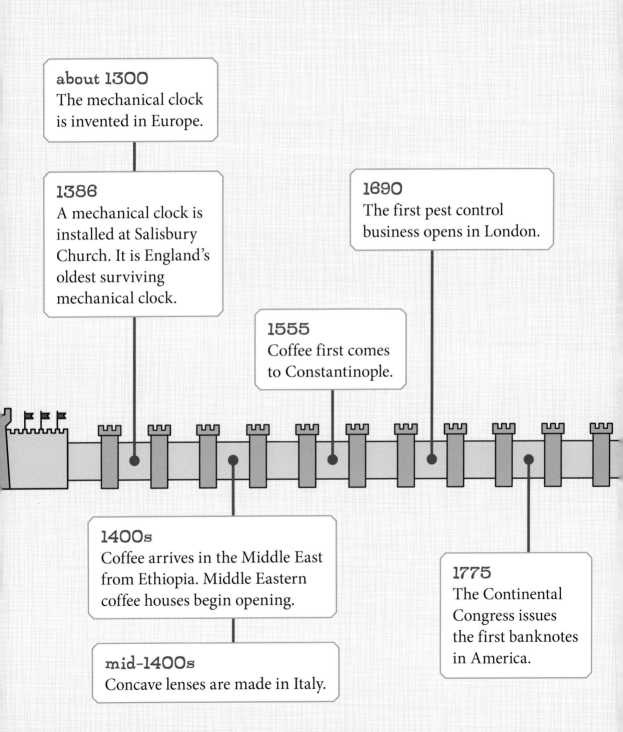

Glossary

cesspit (SESS-pit)—a pit in the ground that holds human waste and other garbage

checkmate (CHEK-mate)—a chess move in which an opponent's king cannot escape

daub (DAWB)—a wet, sticky matter made of wet soil or clay mixed with straw

foliot (FOH-lee-oht)—a horizontal bar with weights at each end; a foliot moves back and forth to help a clock keep time

lord (LORD)—a person of high rank who has great power over other people

lye (LYE)—a strong substance used to make soap

moat (MOHT)—a deep, wide ditch dug all around a castle or fort and filled with water to prevent attacks

monastery (MAH-nuh-ster-ee)—a group of buildings where monks live and work

Muslim (MUHZ-luhm)—a follower of the religion of Islam

noble (NOH-buhl)—a person of wealth and high rank

peasant (PEZ-uhnt)—a farmer who rents land

Persia (PUR-zuh)—ancient empire in southwest Asia founded after 546 BC; name of Iran until 1935

Viking (VYE-king)—a Scandinavian person who attacked parts of Europe between the 8th and 11th centuries

Read More

Roesser, Marie. *The Middle Ages*. New York: Gareth Stevens Publishing, 2020.

Stuckey, Rachel. *Your Guide to Medieval Society*. New York: Crabtree Publishing, 2017.

Vonne, Mora. *Gross Facts About the Middle Ages*. North Mankato, MN: Capstone Press, 2017.

Internet Sites

BBC. Everyday Life in the Middle Ages.
https://www.bbc.co.uk/bitesize/guides/zm4mn39/revision/1

DK Find Out. Castles.
https://www.dkfindout.com/us/history/castles/

Select Bibliography

Ashenburg, Katherine. *The Dirt on Clean: An Unsanitized History*. New York: North Point Press, 2008.

Hoffman, Richard C. *An Environmental History of Medieval Europe*. New York: Cambridge University Press, 2014.

Kurlansky, Mark. *Paper: Paging Through History*. Farmington Hills, MI: Thorndike Press, 2016.

Shenk, David. *The Immortal Game: A History of Chess or How 32 Carved Pieces on a Board Illuminated Our Understanding of War, Art, Science, and the Human Brain*. New York: Doubleday, 2006.

Index

Al-Masaa Café, 20
Arsovic, Goran, 12

bathing, 9, 10, 11

Castile soap, 10
Castile, Spain, 10
cesspits, 28
chamber pots, 28
checkmate, 12, 14
chessboards, 12
China, 34, 41
coffee, 20, 21, 22
Constantinople, 22
Ctesibius, 17

Egypt, 17
Ethiopia, 21, 22

foliots, 19
Franklin, Benjamin, 38

GPS, 32

homes, 6

India, 13

Lebanon, 8
lenses, 36
  bifocal lenses, 38
  concave lenses, 38
  contact lenses, 39
  convex lenses, 37
lodestones, 34
London, England, 23

lords, 6, 7
lye, 8, 10

manors, 6, 7
Mongolia, 42

Nikolic, Ivan, 12
nobles, 14, 18

peasants, 6, 7
Peregrinus, Peter, 34
Persia, 13
pests, 26, 28, 29, 30
  fleas, 30
  mice, 26, 29, 30
  rats, 29, 30, 31

Qatar, 8

rat-catchers, 31

spectacles, 37, 38
sunstones, 33

Time Ball, 16
Times Square, 16

U.S. Bureau of Engraving and Printing, 40

Venice, Italy, 23
Vikings, 33

water clocks, 17
William of Rubruck, 42